HACCP

Carlos H Hernández

HACCP

Concepts & Quick Reference

First Edition in English, 2017

Series: Management Systems

COPYRIGHT Carlos H Hernández

ISBN-13: 978-1977638250
ISBN-10: 1977638252

Content

Introduction. 9

A bit of history. 9

Benefits of the HACCP system 10

HACCP system and its principles. 11

    Principle 1 – Conduct & Hazard Analysis. 12

    Principle 2 – Determine the Critical Control Points. 13

    Principle 3 – Establish Critical Limits. 13

    Principle 4 – Establish Monitoring Procedures. 14

    Principle 5 – Establish Corrective Actions. 15

    Principle 6 – Establish Verification Procedures. 15

    Principle 7 – Establish Records – Keeping and Documentation Procedures. ... 16

Steps to implement a HACCP system 16

    STEP 1 = Form the HACCP team. 16

    STEP 2 = Product Description. 18

    STEP 3 = Intended use. 18

    STEP 4 = Flow Diagrams. 19

    STEP 5 = Confirmation of flowcharts. 21

    STEP 6 = Risk Analysis. 21

    STEP 7 = Determination of CCPs. 24

    STEP 8 = Definition of critical limits. 25

    STEP 9 = Monitoring each CCP. 25

    STEP 10 = Corrective Actions. 26

    STEP 11 = Verification and Validation. 26

    STEP 12 = Documentation. 26

References. 27

Introduction.

Many times out of curiosity or necessity we want to know what HACCP, which means, that concerns, is how it works, what its scope in the world today, what kind of organizations applied, advantages to offer, as it is implemented. Here I present a quick guide that clarifies concepts and a series of steps to implement it.

HACCP is an acronym that is well known in the working environment, but not everyone knows what it really means, in English its meaning is "Hazard Analysis and Critical Control Point". It is a system that allows you to identify specific hazards and implement measures to its control and mitigation in order to ensure the safety of foods or packaging containing food. It is a tool to evaluate the hazards and establish control systems that ensure prevention instead of relying on the final product inspection.

The HACCP system can be applied throughout the food, starting in primary producer to final consumer chain, and its application should be based on scientific evidence of hazards to human health, as well as improving the safety of food, the application of the HACCP system can offer significant advantages and promote international trade to boost confidence in the safety of food.

Today, the majority of management systems are compatible, easily integrating among them, in my experience, the basic system in which all systems are integrated is in the quality management system based on the ISO 9000 standard.

A bit of history.

The HACCP system was developed in 1971 by H.E. Bauman originally by the company Pillsbury, NASA and the laboratory Natick of the Navy of the United States in the 1960s, as a response to the requirements imposed by NASA food safety for food processing free of any origin viral, bacterial or any other pathogen for astronauts on space flights.

Thus began the operational management of the Pillsbury Company, who in their search for a more efficient system in the safety of their food, began by modifying this program, making preventive nature in order to make it fully effective at NASA, being basically changes that occurred the following:

- Control the raw material
- Production environment control
- Process Control.

Then make revisions and refinements, the food Codex provided a description and application of the HACCP principles, recognized internationally as an effective system for monitoring food safety.

This perspective in 1971 the HACCP system was presented as a novelty at the National Conference of protection of the food of the United States, and was the Food and Drug Administration - FDA, which I adopt this concept and use this system as a framework General to establish regulations based on HACCP.

Benefits of the HACCP system.

- Assure that the products we consume are harmless and safe and effective processes.
- Reduction of claims, returns, reprocesses, rejections and withdrawals from the market.
- It is a Marketing tool, because it gives a good image of credibility for the establishment, exploiting it as a competitive advantage that others do not have.
- Decrease in costs and saving resources.
- Optimal prevention of diseases transmitted by food (DTF´s).
- It provides evidence of a safe and efficient handling of food or food packaging.
- The company's position.
- Growing awareness of labor quality among employees.
- Increase in the level of training of the personnel.
- Level rise in that customers are satisfied.
- Eliminate barriers to international trade.

HACCP system and its principles.

HACCP is a system that can diagram in the following way:

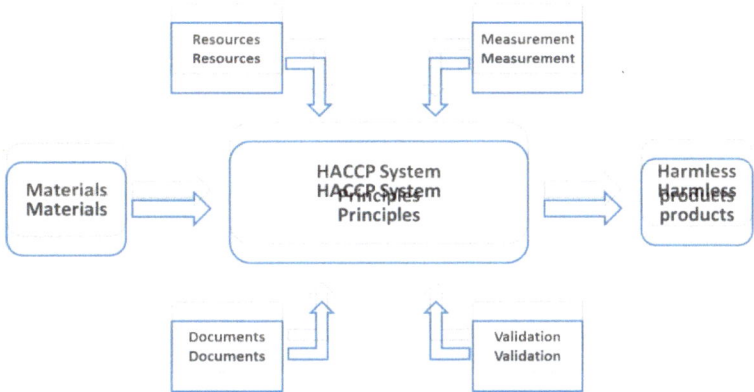

HACCP is a system that identifies specific hazards and preventive measures for its control. This system is based on the seven principles which we can say that they are his philosophy or bases on which it is based.

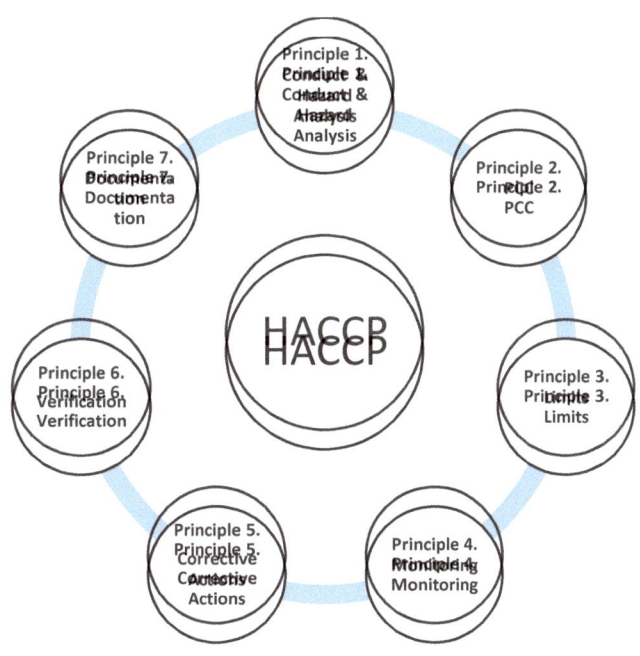

Principle 1 – Conduct & Hazard Analysis.

First of all, we have to be clear about the difference between a hazard and a risk:

Hazard: Any physical, chemical, or biological agent that can contaminate food. In other words the potential something that can be a source of contamination

Risk: This is the probability that appears one of the dangers in combination with the severity of the damage they can cause to the consumer in case that materializes an incident or event.

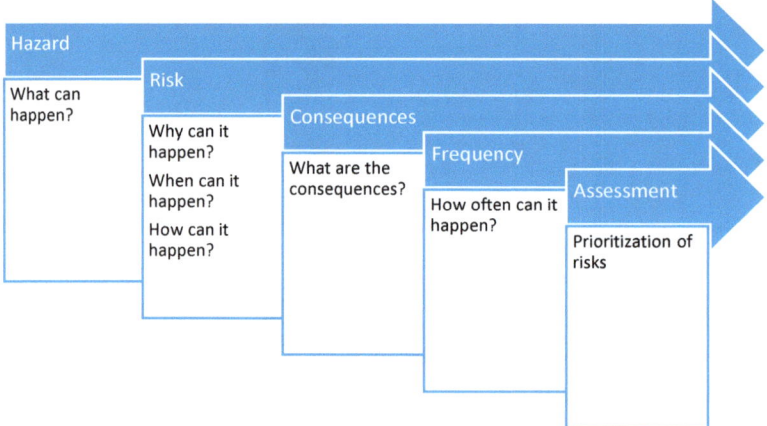

The analysis of hazards and risks starts from receipt of materials until the delivery of the finished products to the client. To carry out this analysis there are many techniques, the most used are: checklists, historical analysis of incidents/accidents, analysis of the modes of failure and effect.

Some of the dangers that we find in the food industry are detailed below:

Physical agent	Foreign objects in food, Unsafe transport conditions (internal and external) and holds (internal and external), Damaged packaging material, Not suitable cleaning conditions, Poor sealing of boxes or containers.
Chemical Agent	Presence of powders, Odors, Chemicals, Organic matter, Fats and Lubricants.
Biological Agent	Presence of pests, Mismanagement of waste, Microorganisms due to lack of hygiene of facilities and personnel, Unfiltered process air, Pathogens in water, Toxins generated by certain foods.
Allergens	Their presence makes them a danger to groups of consumers who do not tolerate it.

Principle 2 – Determine the Critical Control Points.

According to Codex a Critical Control Point is defined as "A stage where control can be applied and is essential to avoid or eliminate a food safety hazard or to reduce it to an acceptable level."

We must bear in mind the difference between a Control Point and a Critical Control Point, its main difference being that a PC not necessarily being out of control implies a danger to food safety, but if it were PCC would clearly mean a danger for being critical, but both must be controlled.

Critical control points should be determined if any.

Principle 3 – Establish Critical Limits.

By definition a critical limit is a criterion that differentiates the acceptability or unacceptability of the process in a given phase.

Critical Limits
A critical limit represents the limits used to judge whether a product is harmless or not. Critical limits can be set for factors such as temperature, time, physical dimensions of the product, water activity, moisture level, colorants, etc. These parameters, when kept within the limits, confirm the safety of the food.

Operational limits
If process and equipment control or critical limit monitoring show a tendency toward loss of control of a CCP, operators can avoid it before critical threshold deviations occur. The value of the parameter in question is called "operational limit".
Operational limits are generally more restrictive and are set at a level reached before the critical limit is violated. That is, they should avoid deviations from critical limits that mean lack of control of the hazard.

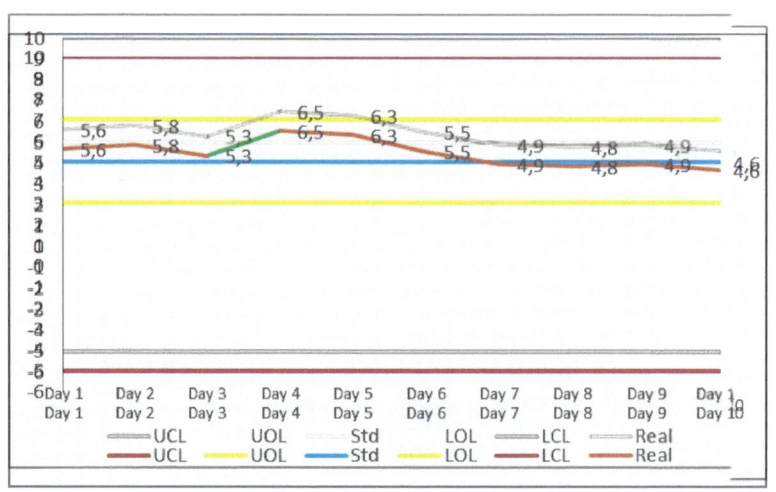

Statistical control to show the behavior of a temperature variable °C within its upper and lower operating limits and critical limits.

Principle 4 – Establish Monitoring Procedures.

The Guidelines for the Implementation of the Codex HACCP System define monitoring as "the act of performing a planned sequence of observations or measures of control parameters to assess whether a CCP is under control." The planned sequence should preferably result in specific procedures for the monitoring in question:

Monitoring procedures should detect the loss of control of a CCP, in time to avoid the production of an unsafe food or to interrupt the process. Complete, how, when and by whom monitoring will be performed. Each organization decides how to carry out the monitoring depending on its resources and criticality. Monitoring can be done continuously, selectively or by production batches.

A well-known way is to monitor the CCPs with a control plan, which specifies what will be monitored, how will the critical limits be monitored, what will be the frequency of monitoring, who will monitor, where monitored? And what will be the performance in case of a diversion.

All equipment used for monitoring must be calibrated at defined intervals according to the use and characteristics of the measuring equipment.

Principle 5 – Establish Corrective Actions.

Guidelines for application of system HACCP Codex define corrective action as "any action to be taken, when the results of the monitoring the CCP indicate a loss of control":

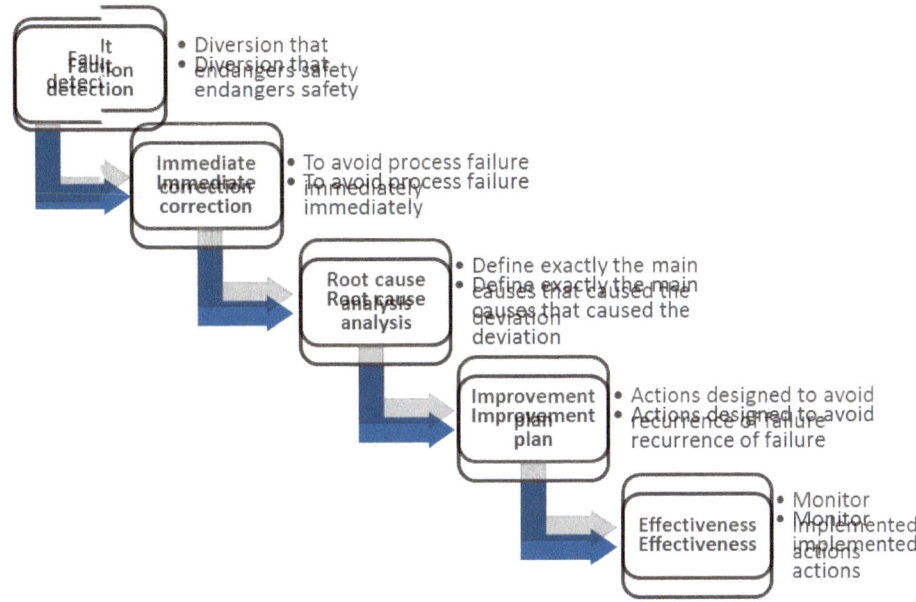

Principle 6 – Establish Verification Procedures.

The Codex guidelines define verification as "the application of methods, procedures, tests and other assessments, as well as monitoring, to determine compliance with the HACCP plan."

Verification should be made periodically, whenever there is any change in products, ingredients, packaging, processes, deviations, claims. Verifications can be done with qualified internal or external personnel.

Principle 7 – Establish Records – Keeping and Documentation Procedures.

Establish a system of documentation on all procedures and records appropriate to these principles and their application.

The documentation covers manuals, specifications of materials, laws and local and national government regulations to which the products are directed, listing, recipes, procedures, records; any document related to the process and product.

The documentation must be in the language spoken in the organization, ensure that the documents are within reach of the operative parts and are easy to retrieve.

Four types of records must be maintained as part of the system:
- Supporting documentation.
- Records generated.
- Documentation of methods, procedures and instructions.
- Training records.

Steps to implement a HACCP system

STEP 1 - Form the HACCP team.

The HACCP team will be in charge of designing and implementing the system. This team preferably has to be multidisciplinary and must have previous experience and extensive knowledge of the product and the process. It is necessary that these people receive training and that they read in its entirety this text. The recommended training or training should cover the following areas: Quality assurance and control, Food technology and packaging, Microbiological analysis (food microbiology) and hazards and physical-chemical analysis, Knowledge of machinery and process equipment.

The HACCP equipment is outlined in the following table:

Full name	Position in the organization	Position in the team	Responsibilities in the team
		Team leader	<ul><li>Leader of the HACCP team.</li><li>Chair the meetings of the HACCP team.</li><li>Provide resources for the implementation and implementation of HACCP.</li><li>Promote the continuity of HACCP.</li><li>Communication of process changes within the company and with customers.</li></ul>
		Responsible for the production plant or process	<ul><li>Verify compliance with process parameters.</li><li>Evaluate the requirements of raw material and inputs.</li><li>Inform operations management of production reports.</li><li>Verify that the storage conditions of finished materials and products are adequate.</li></ul>
		Maintenance of facilities, machinery and equipment	<ul><li>Schedule and enforce the preventive and corrective maintenance of facilities, machinery and equipment.</li></ul>
		Human Resources	<ul><li>Coordinate with the Production Manager / Plant Manager to provide the training and training.</li><li>Ensure compliance with the contagious / infectious diseases program.</li><li>Document the use of personal protective equipment according to the circumstances.</li></ul>
		Assurance and Quality Control (HACCP System Coordinator)	<ul><li>Responsible for the monitoring and daily control of the HACCP plan, through the monitoring of the process.</li><li>Report product defects and failures.</li><li>Sign and review the records of the HACCP system.</li><li>Enforce cleanliness and hygiene procedures.</li><li>Follow-up on safety indicators.</li><li>Coordinate the performance of required microbiological analyzes.</li><li>Verify compliance with the foreign object management program.</li></ul>
		Inspector of Safety	<ul><li>Follow up to the quality control plan.</li><li>Verify that all material and finished product specifications are current.</li><li>Verify that the quality equipment is updated in its calibration.</li><li>Predict and verify the cleaning of equipment, machinery and plant facilities. Responsible for the monitoring of the HACCP Plan.</li><li>Evaluate compliance with Good Manufacturing Practices.</li><li>Monitoring of pest control.</li></ul>

The responsibilities presented in the table above are generic. It will have to be specific depending on the organization.

The team must be authorized by the highest authority of the operation or who is designated for approval.

STEP 2 - Product Description.

The product characteristics must be clearly defined, a complete description must be given, its ingredients - never forgetting the additives - and additional information regarding its safety and stability. The product must be defined including at least the following parameters: composition, manufacturing process, presentation and format, shelf life, storage and distribution conditions.

Product:	Trade name as the product is known by customers and consumers.
Description:	Detailed Product Description.
Composition:	Fully describe the physic-chemical composition.
Presentation and format:	Sizes in which the product is sold, as well as a description of the packaging.
Shelf life:	Shelf life, days, weeks or months.
Storage and distribution conditions:	As stored, humidity and temperature conditions, indoor or outdoor, it should be mixed with other products, on pallets, stack of packages.

STEP 3 – intended use.

Normal use which makes customer or consumer of the product, i.e. If eat it raw, cooked, combined with other foods, thawed, if packing material as applies it must be defined. You have clear types of consumers toward that target. A basic manual with information on its mode of preparation, management and conservation is also required if necessary.

Expected use:	How the product will be consumed or used.
Objective market:	If it is for industrial use or final consumption. Types of consumers, all public or there are restrictions. If you carry an allergen it must be declared according to the regulations of the country where it will be consumed.
Instructions for use:	It will be used cold, hot or needs to be tempered before use: If it is for industrial use specify the type of process where it can be used.

STEP 4 - Flow Diagrams.

Flow diagrams need to be made real, with the support of operational staff, flow charts are key in hazard analysis. The diagrams go from the reception of raw material to the delivery of the product to the customer, must be exactly defined to where our responsibility comes.

To begin this process, the first thing to do is to analyze the flow of processes, have defined areas of raw material storage, chemical storage, storage of materials and packaging materials, processing and reprocessing areas, product warehouse finished, dispatch area, etc. In order to visualize how the flow of materials is developed.

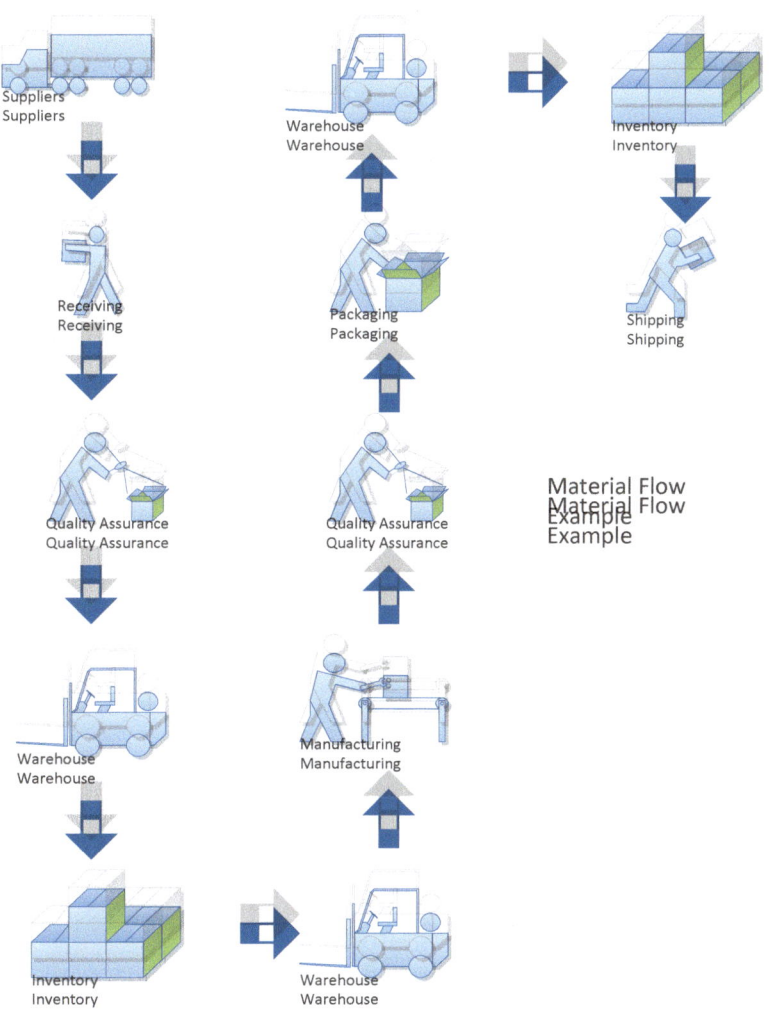

Material Flow Example

Now the next activity is the elaboration of the flow charts, you can use many different nomenclatures but the following give very good result:

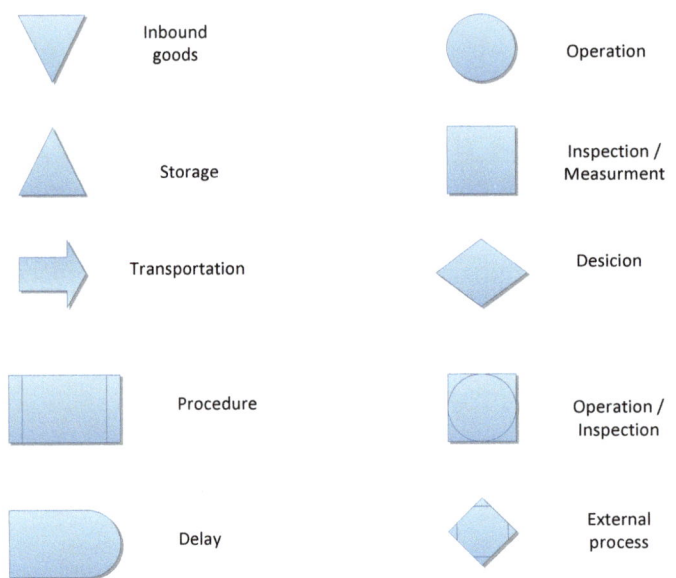

The flow diagrams must demonstrate their interconnectivity between the main processes and detail the process itself, see the following example:

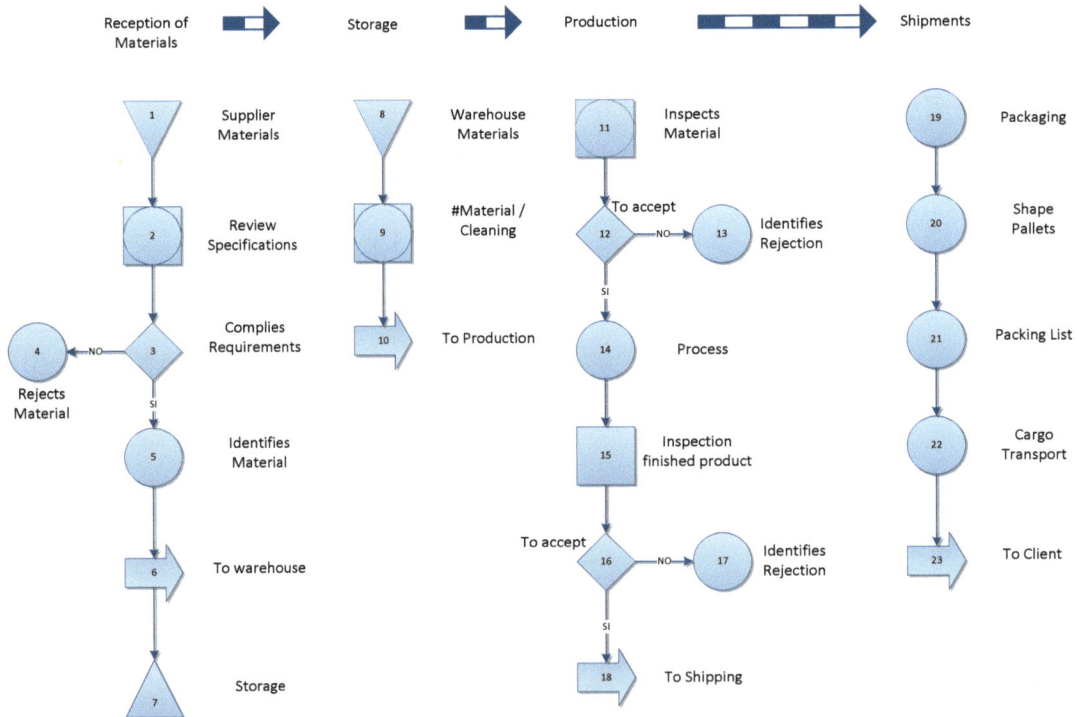

STEP 5 - Confirmation of flowcharts.

The HACCP team should visit the plant to confirm that all operations were correctly included in the flowchart. It will be checked directly with the process operators, they must guarantee each activity.

It is advisable to confirm for each product and to place a date for each revision. Reviews are mandated to exist at some change within the process (machinery, materials, temperatures, time, speeds, etc.).

STEP 6 - Risk Analysis.

It consists of identifying the potential hazards associated with each of the different phases of the production process, packing, storing materials, assessing the likelihood of such hazards occurring and identifying preventive measures necessary for their control. The risks and dangers of the production process will be evaluated for each of the ingredients and stages of the process from its developed flow chart.
An individual risk analysis should be done for each particular product.

a) Define methodology to assess the criticality of each risk.

Qualitative analysis of criticality

Examples for primary packaging of a product, these tables depend exclusively on the product being analyzed.

Probability of Occurrence

Probability	Value	Explanation
High	4	Occurs frequently, weekly or monthly
Half	3	Occurs rarely, less than one year
Low	2	Almost never happens, one to five years
Insignificant	1	It has never happened, more than 5 years

Severity in health

Severity	Value	Damage to health
High	4	A part of the packaging that is peeled towards the food and may cause choking or damage to the consumer.
Half	3	There is a defect in the lid that affects the product and / or the consumer (eg high level of a component that can affect organoleptically the beverage or use of toxic product not suitable for food use)
Low	2	There is a defect in the lid that does not affect the product or the consumer (e.g. black spots and spots that cannot reach the liquid, deformation)
Insignificant	1	There are no defects in the lid that does not affect the product or the consumer (e.g. broken or badly sealed boxes)

Criticality of risk

	Probability			
Severity	High(4)	Half(3)	Low(2)	Insignificant(1)
High(4)	16	12	8	4
Half(3)	12	9	6	3
Low(2)	8	6	4	2
Insignificant(1)	4	3	2	1

b) Identify all potential risks associated with each step of the process

Potential risks are analyzed following the flow chart and can be detailed in the following table:

N⁰	Activity	Risk	Risk Description	Operational control	Severity	Probability	Criticality of risk	Adverse health effects	Control Measure
①	②	③	④	⑤	⑥	⑦	⑧	⑨	⑩

1: Activity number corresponding to the flowchart.
2: Name of the activity and its description.
3: Evaluate the risk from the physical, chemical and biological point of view; put your F, Q or B identification in the cell.
4: Describe the risk in as much detail as possible.
5: Procedure, instructive, method of working with is controlled or minimized risk.

c) Evaluate each potential risk

6: Assign the value of severity that can cause the products failed based on the table "Severity in health".
7: Probability that the event occurs or has occurred in the past, table "Probability of occurrence".
8: In table "Criticist of risk", cross the value of Severity and Probability to find the value of criticality.

d) Determine the control measures of each risk

9: Clearly describe the adverse effect on consumer health.
10: Detail if it is necessary to implement an additional control measure.

Each activity depending on its complexity can have physical, chemical and biological risks at the same time or only part of them.

STEP 7 - Determination of CCPs.

A CCP is a stage that can be controlled and as a result prevents, eliminates or reduces to an acceptable level a risk that can affect the health of the consumer. The PCC must be justifiable, validated and measurable.

Decision Tree for Determination of Critical Control Points

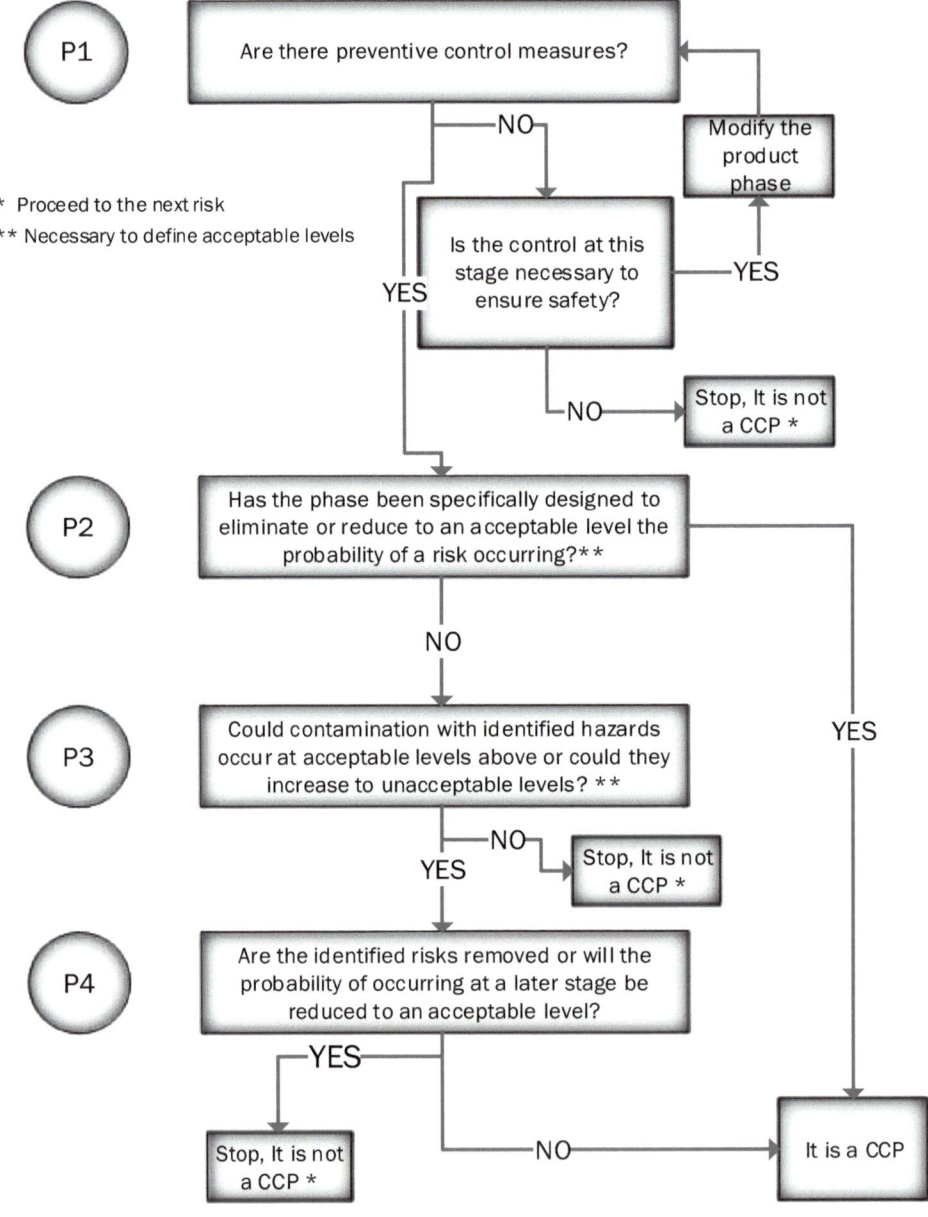

* Proceed to the next risk
** Necessary to define acceptable levels

Each risk is evaluated with these 4 questions and we define the CCPs, for that we can support in the following table:

No	Activity	Decision tree questions				CCP
		P1	P2	P3	P4	
①	②	③	④	⑤	⑥	⑦

①: Activity number corresponding to the flowchart.
②: Name of the activity and its description.
③: Answer Y / N of Question 1.
④: Answer Y / N of Question 2.
⑤: Answer Y / N of Question 3.
⑥: Answer Y / N of Question 4.
⑦: Y / N answer assuring if it is a CCP.

STEP 8 - Definition of critical limits.

A critical limit is the maximum and / or minimum value of a biological, physical or chemical parameter that must be controlled in the CCP. The objective of the Critical Limit is to ensure control of the CCP so that it is possible to determine when it is out of control.

STEP 9 - Monitoring each CCP.

Monitoring: planned sequence of observations or measurements to determine if a CCP is under control and to deliver detailed records that will then be used for verification.

To have a better visualization, the CCPs monitor them through a CCP Control Plan detailed below:

CCP	Significant risks	Monitoring				Registers	Verification
		What	How	Frequency	Who		
i	ii	iii	iv	v	vi	vii	viii

i : Identification or name of the CCP.
ii : Risks associated with deviation beyond control, detected in risk analysis, can be physical, chemical or biological.
iii : That is monitored.
iv : How it is monitored.
v : When Monitored.
vi : What monitors.
vii : Records showing evidence that CCP is controlled.
viii : Who checks? That everything is done to keep the CCP in control.

STEP 10 - Corrective Actions.

It is defined as the procedures that must be implemented when a deviation occurs.

If a HACCP plan is designed and implemented properly, all deviations will be recorded and appropriate corrective actions will be taken prior to release of the product.

STEP 11 - Verification and Validation.

Verification: Those activities, which are not monitoring but which determine the validity of the HACCP plan, activities that do not belong to HACCP must be verified and always controlled through the Operational Control.

Validation: seeks to collect and evaluate technical and scientific information, in order to determine if the HACCP plan is effectively controlling the risks. It should be checked at a stipulated or mandatory frequency if there is a change in materials, processes, equipment, formulations, etc.

STEP 12 - Documentation.

The records are written evidence through which an act is documented. HACCP documentation must be included as part of the organization's product release and must be reviewed by the HACCP coordinator. Product release must include confirmation that no deviations occurred.

References

http://www.fao.org/fao-who-codexalimentarius/en/

About the Author:

CARLOS H HERNANDEZ, Systems Engineer with experience in the management of industrial plants and plastic primary packaging for the beverage industry, post-graduate studies in Business Administration, Risk Prevention and Project Management. Extensive experience in consulting and implementation of management systems based on ISO Standards, as well as Leader Auditor for ISO 9001, 14001, 22000 and OHSAS 18001 standards as well as university professor and business trainer.

www.ingramcontent.com/pod-product-compliance
Lightning Source LLC
Chambersburg PA
CBHW051942210526
45473CB00006B/2352